I Can Be Anythir

I CAN BE
DOCTOR

By Audrey Charles

Gareth Stevens
PUBLISHING

Please visit our website, www.garethstevens.com. For a free color catalog of all our high-quality books, call toll free 1-800-542-2595 or fax 1-877-542-2596.

Cataloging-in-Publication Data

Names: Charles, Audrey.
Title: I can be a doctor / Audrey Charles.
Description: New York : Gareth Stevens Publishing, 2018. | Series: I can be anything! | Includes index.
Identifiers: ISBN 9781482463170 (pbk.) | ISBN 9781482463194 (library bound) | ISBN 9781482463187 (6 pack)
Subjects: LCSH: Medicine–Vocational guidance–Juvenile literature. | Physicians–Juvenile literature.
Classification: LCC R690.C43 2018 | DDC 610.69–dc23

First Edition

Published in 2018 by
Gareth Stevens Publishing
111 East 14th Street, Suite 349
New York, NY 10003

Copyright © 2018 Gareth Stevens Publishing

Editor: Therese Shea
Designer: Sarah Liddell

Photo credits: Cover, p. 1 (kid) Santiago Cornejo/Shutterstock.com; cover, p. 1 (background) Rob Byron/Shutterstock.com; pp. 5, 11, 13, 15, 17, 19, 21, 24 (both) luckyraccoon/Shutterstock.com; p. 7 VGstockstudio/Shutterstock.com; p. 9 Africa Studio/Shutterstock.com; p. 23 hin255/Shutterstock.com.

Printed in the United States of America

CPSIA compliance information: Batch #CS17GS: For further information contact Gareth Stevens, New York, New York at 1-800-542-2595.

Contents

Dr. Jones is
a pediatrician.
That means she is
a children's doctor.

She helped
my friend Mary.
Mary hurt her leg.

Dr. Jones helped my brother John. John had a cold.

I go to see Dr. Jones.
I need a checkup.

Dr. Jones listens
to my heart.
It beats like a drum!

She looks in my ears.
They are healthy!

She looks in my mouth.
I say, "Ahh!"

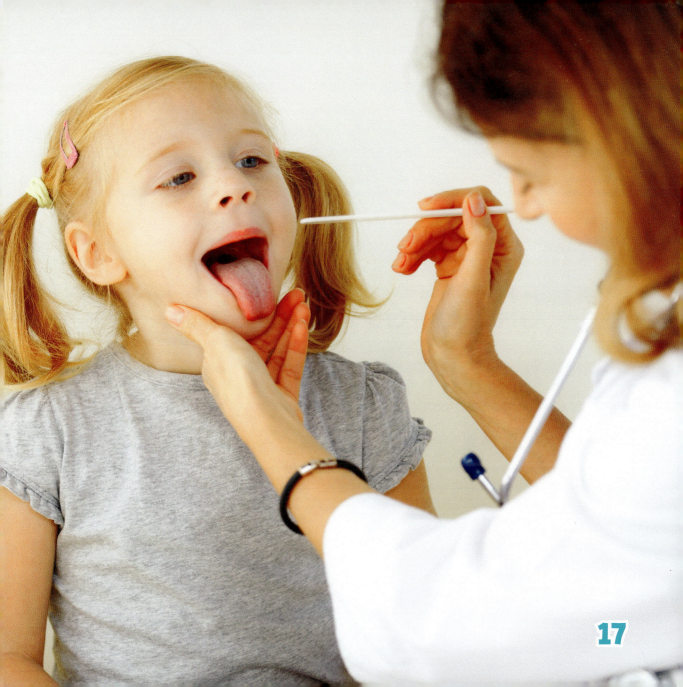

She gives me a shot.
It didn't hurt!

I want to help
people, too.
I want to be a doctor!

I can be a doctor.
So can you!

Words to Know

pediatrician

shot

Index